THE BRAI...

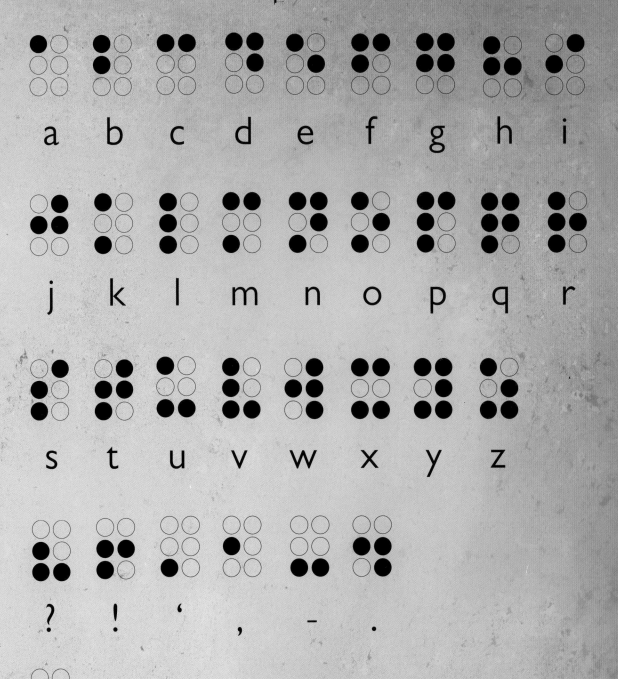

capital

The capital sign placed before a letter makes it a capital letter.

number

The number sign placed before the letters a–j makes the numbers 1–9 and 0.

PRONUNCIATION GUIDE
for French words, names, and phrases used in the text

Louis Braille (loo-WEE brale)

Papa (pah-PAH)

Maman (mah-MAHN)

Coupvray (koo-VRAY)

N'y touche pas! (nee toosh PAH)

Marquise (mar-KEEZ)

Bienvenue! (byehn-veh-NOO)

Paris (pah-REE)

Gabriel (gah-bree-EL)

Asseyez-vous ici! (ah-SAY-ay-voo ee-SEE)

Voilà! (vwah-LAH)

C'est tout? (say TOO)

Lève-toi! (lev-TWAH)

Allons! (ah-LOHNZ)

Pignier (peen-YAY)

Oui! (wee)

Fini! (fih-NEE)

Tu l'as fait! (too lah FAY)

Si facile! (see fah-SEEL)

Et si vite! (eh see VEET)

SIX DOTS

A STORY OF YOUNG LOUIS BRAILLE

BY

JEN BRYANT

ILLUSTRATIONS BY

BORIS KULIKOV

Alfred A. Knopf · New York

On the day I was born, Papa announced me
to the village: "Here is my son Loo-WEE!"
The neighbors came, clucking their tongues, whispering:
"Too small. He won't survive!"

Oh, but I *did* survive.
I was a curious child, and my eyes studied everything:
Maman's gentle face. Lace draping my cradle.
The smooth shape of a bread loaf on the table.

I grew strong and healthy.
When I rode to the baker's on my brother's broad
shoulders or fed the chickens with my sisters,
the villagers waved and smiled.
"So handsome!" they cried.

"And clever, too," my sisters said.
At three, I knew everyone in Coupvray by name.
I counted the eggs in my sister's basket
and the sparrows in the trees. I repeated stories
I heard, word for word.

But what I loved most was to watch Papa work.
People came from far away to have a harness made
or a broken bridle mended. In Papa's hands, the rough leather strips
became smooth and useful.

I wanted to be just like him.
But when I reached for a tool . . .
N'y touche pas! "Don't touch that!" Papa warned.
Then, more gently: "You're too small yet, Louis.
Wait till you're older."

Too small . . . Those words!
I wanted to be bigger, stronger, older.
Perhaps if I showed Papa what I could do . . .

The leather was smooth. The awl was sharp.
I knew just how to—

"Papa! Papa!!! PaPAAAAAAAAAAAAAAAA!"

My life changed that day.
A healer bandaged my eye.
Again, I heard: *N'y touche pas!* "Don't touch!"

But the bandage itched so much!
My hands, like the sparrows in the trees, were small and quick.
I couldn't keep them away.
I didn't *mean* to make things worse. But—
I did.
The infection spread to my other eye, until . . .

. . . I could see nothing at all. No trees or sparrows.
No faces. No lace or loaves of bread.
By the time I turned five, I was completely blind.

The villagers whispered: "Poor Louis Braille!
Such a clever boy.
What will happen to him now?"

My world was dark and dangerous.
I stumbled about the house, banging into the chairs,
the walls, the door. My body ached.
"Where is the sun?!" I cried.

But the sun did not come. I sat by the window,
training my ears to do what my eyes could not.

Clang, bang, kish, kish
—that was Papa in his shop.

Swoosh, swish, swoosh, swish
—long-skirted ladies hurrying to market.

Clomp, clomp, clomp, stomp
—soldiers marching down the street.

*Grrrrr, grrrrr,
ruff, rrrrruff!
GRRRRRR*

—the neighbor's angry dog, chained too tight.
Alone in the dark . . .

I knew just
how he felt!

My family did what they could.
Papa made a wooden cane.
Each day I walked a little farther, *tap-tap, tap-tap, tap-tap* . . .
counting the steps between the house and the garden,
the vineyard and the chicken coop,
the baker's and the miller's . . .
and back to Papa's shop.

My brother taught me to whistle:
vreeee, vreeee, vreeeew!
And when the sound echoed back,
it warned me of things in my path.

My sisters made a straw alphabet.
Papa made letters with leather strips
or by pounding round-topped
nails into boards.

With Maman, I played dominoes,
counting the dots with my fingertips.

The village priest taught me to recognize trees by their touch,
flowers by their scent, and birds by their song.
I listened closely as he read to me
from the Bible and from books of poetry.

"Do you have books for blind children?" I asked.
"No, Louis," the priest replied. "I'm sorry."

When I was older, I went to school with the other village children.
All day, as they wrote down words and numbers
or read out loud from printed pages,
I sat in the front row, listening and memorizing.

"Do you have books for blind children?" I asked again.
"No, Louis," the teacher replied. "I'm sorry."

But I didn't want people
to feel sorry for me.
I just wanted to read and
to write on my own,
like everyone else.

The Marquise, a noble lady living nearby, heard about me.
She wrote a letter to the Royal School for the Blind,
asking if I could study there.
Finally, a reply came. *Bienvenue!* "Welcome, Louis!"

"The priest says they have books for the blind!" I told Papa excitedly.
"But you're only *ten*!" Maman cried.
"And you'll live there most of the year," my brother added.
"Paris is a big city, far away!" my sisters warned.

How could I make them understand? Without books,
I would always be "poor Louis Braille." I would always be
held back, like that dog chained too tight.
"I love you," I told them.
"But I must go."

I didn't need my eyes to know
that the Royal School in Paris was *not* a palace!
My hard bed was in a damp, crowded room.
My uniform itched. My meals were small and cold.
The teachers were strict. The older boys teased and stole.
How I missed my home!

And yet . . . I stayed. I stayed because somewhere in this old,
moldy building, there were books for the blind.
"Only the best students are allowed to read them,"
my friend Gabriel told me.
"Then I will be one of the best," I replied.

Learning at the blind school was almost like learning
in Coupvray: We sat and listened. We memorized and recited.
We also had music lessons and made slippers in the workshop.
As my fingers flew across the organ keys or between
the strips of cloth, I dreamed of reading and writing.

I worked and studied as hard as I could. Finally . . .

. . . it was THAT day.
A guide led me to the library.
Asseyez-vous ici! "Sit here!" he commanded.
There was shuffling, grunting, and scraping.
A *thud.*

Voilà! "There it is," he said.
"Just trace the raised letters with your fingers."
It was a long reach to the top of page one.
My fingers traced the outline of each letter,
just as I'd done in Coupvray, with straw and leather.

But these waxy letters were huge! After "reading" the first sentence
this way, my hand was halfway down the page.
A few sentences more, and I had to *turn* the page.
A few more sentences. Two more pages.
And then . . . the end!

C'est tout? "Is that all?" I asked.

"There are more," the guide replied. "But they're just like this one."

Words as large as my hand! Sentences that took up half a page!

I sighed. Even if I read a hundred books like this,

how much could I learn?

I skipped supper. I lay in bed, wishing I was home.
When I finally fell asleep, I dreamed that the neighbor's angry dog . . .
broke free. He ran to me, licking my face until I laughed
and laughed.

"Louis, Louis!" *Lève-toi!* "Get up!"
Gabriel shook me awake. It was morning.
"The headmaster wants us. Let's go!" *Allons!*

Everyone had gathered in the big room.
Dr. Pignier spoke: "A French army captain has
invented a code to send secret messages
during battle. The code is read by touch,
not by sight, so we might use it here, too."

"You're each holding a message, written with patterns
of dots," the headmaster continued.
"Each pattern stands for a sound, such as -*ou* or -*in* or -*ch*."

We listened as he explained.
It wasn't easy. There was *a lot* to remember.
Flipping my paper over, I moved my fingers
from left to right, feeling the dots.
"Fall back!" I shouted.

Everyone laughed. It was a battle order, of course!
But now my heart pounded with hope.
I asked for another.

Again, I touched the dots. "Supplies arrive at dawn."
Oui! "Yes!" the headmaster cried.
The others shouted out their messages, too.

"How are the messages *written*?" I asked.
The headmaster handed me a slate: a wooden frame with a metal piece
in the middle. "Slide your paper underneath," he explained.
"Now take this stylus . . . but be careful!"

The sharp tool was like the awl in Papa's shop. I shivered.

"Use it to punch the code into the paper," he said.
I made a few of the complicated dot patterns, then
flipped the paper to read them by touch.

For many weeks, I practiced.
Reading by touch using dots was a brilliant idea—
at least on the battlefield. But for us? The code was so hard
that everyone else in the school had given up.

"Even a short message takes so *many* dots,
and I can't fit a single symbol under my finger!"
I complained to Gabriel.
"Plus . . . the captain's code stands for *sounds*, not for letters."

"So what?" my friend replied.
"So—why shouldn't we spell words and write sentences
like sighted people do?" I argued.

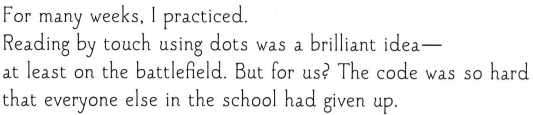

This code was a start. But it wasn't nearly good enough.
We, the blind, were still held back.
"Would the captain work on improving it with me?"
I asked the headmaster.

"I'm sorry, Louis.
He isn't interested," he replied.
Sorry . . . That word!

Long ago, I had watched Papa take rough leather strips
and make them useful.
Now I knew what I had to do.
Late at night, while the others slept, I bent over my slate
and punched the pages. I tried hundreds of ways
to simplify the captain's code.
I worked until my back was stiff and my fingers ached.
Often, I fell asleep a few minutes before morning.

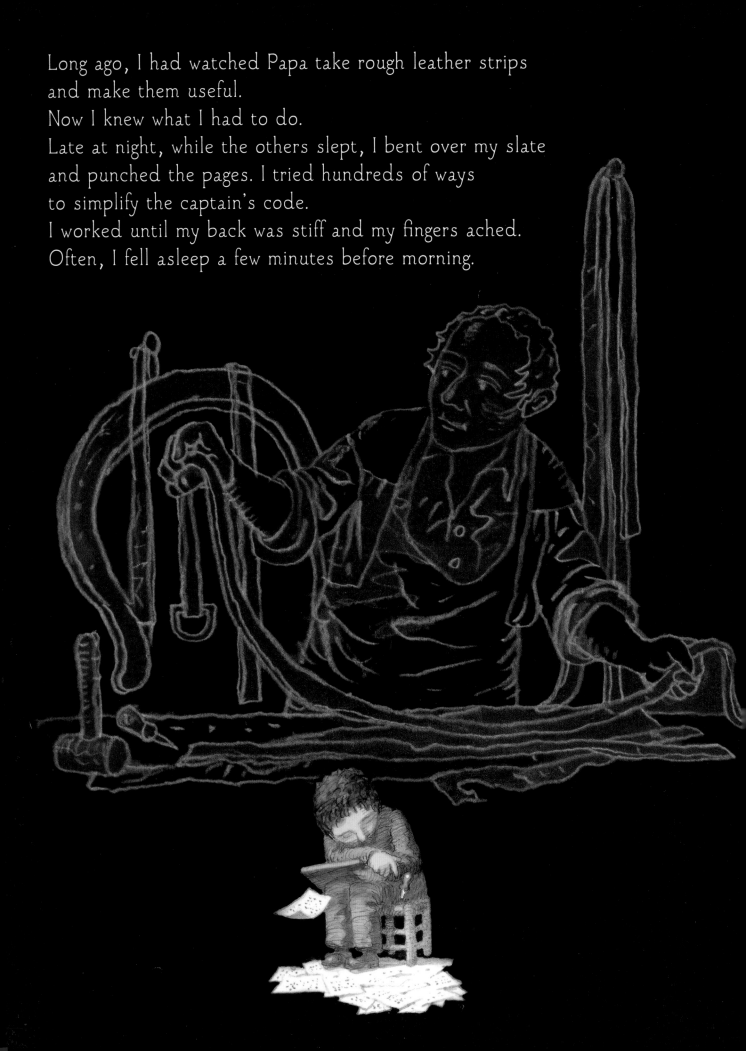

A year passed. Then another. And another.
That winter, I turned fifteen. I was often sick.
But I wouldn't rest.

Finally, it was ready to test.
I asked the headmaster to choose something from
his own library, a book I'd never heard of before.
"Please, read it out loud," I said.

Dr. Pignier began. After a few minutes,
I interrupted. "You can go much faster, sir."
As he read, I copied down the words,
spelling each one correctly.

My new code used just six dots,
arranged in two columns, like dominoes.
Each dot pattern stood for a letter of the alphabet.

Fini! said Dr. Pignier when he reached the end of chapter one.
"Finished!"

I turned my pages over. Reading by touch,
I recited the entire chapter.

Louis, tu l'as fait! "You did it!" he shouted.

Word spread quickly. The other students rushed to try it.
Si facile! "So easy!"
Et si vite! "And so fast!"
"We can read words and write letters like everyone else."

As my friends traded messages, I remembered
watching Papa in his shop,
bent over rough strips of leather, making them useful.

I had become like him, after all.

AUTHOR'S NOTE

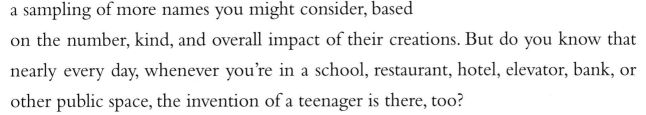

If I asked you to make a list of great inventors, who would be on that list? Gutenberg? Da Vinci? Edison? Then there are Bell, Franklin, Marconi, Tesla, Carver, Whitney, Hopper—just a sampling of more names you might consider, based on the number, kind, and overall impact of their creations. But do you know that nearly every day, whenever you're in a school, restaurant, hotel, elevator, bank, or other public space, the invention of a teenager is there, too?

The name Braille deserves to be on everyone's list of great inventors. Just like these others, he recognized a rough idea (a fingertip code used on battlefields) and worked exhaustively to shape it into something that changed the world forever. Unlike those other inventors, however, Braille was a *child* inventor who worked alone and without public support or financial backing. Living in a converted prison building and already suffering the early signs of lung disease, Louis Braille managed to create a system of reading and writing for the blind that is still used today. In the past several centuries, no one so young has developed something that has had such a lasting and profound impact on so many people.

This is my second book about Louis Braille. In 1994, my young adult biography of Braille was published as part of the series Great Achievers: Lives of the Physically Challenged. The book was designed to inform, and it did so well enough, I think. But more recently, as I encountered examples of the Braille alphabet in public libraries and on college campuses, in airports and on ATMs, I asked myself: What did it FEEL like to be Louis Braille? Nothing I'd read about the young Frenchman, including my own account, had led me to experience Braille's emotions. What was it like to BE Louis Braille? This story is my attempt to answer these questions.

MORE ABOUT BRAILLE:

Q: Why was Louis's invention of Braille so important?

A: Helen Keller compared Braille to Gutenberg, the inventor of the printing press. Before Gutenberg, literacy (reading and writing) belonged to a select few. Millions of ordinary people were, for the most part, left out. But then came the printing press and suddenly everyone had access to books—and the freedom to learn, to exchange ideas, and to improve their lives. The same is true for Louis's invention: Before Braille, the blind were shut off from reading and writing. The Braille system changed all that.

Q: The Braille family showed courage and empathy toward Louis. Was that unusual?

A: Yes, it surely was. In the early 1800s, a family's survival depended on its members doing their share of daily labor. Blind, deaf, or otherwise physically challenged children were often abandoned or given over to a traveling "master," who taught them to sing, dance, or perform tricks for money, much like circus animals. Determined that Louis would avoid such a fate, his family encouraged his independence and education.

Q: What changes did Louis make to the Braille system after his first demonstration?

A: The earliest version of Louis's code included a few of the dashes that Captain Charles Barbier's original "night writing" system had also used. But as Louis continued to refine it, he eliminated the dashes and added numbers, punctuation, and musical notation. By 1829, five years after he showed his work to Dr. André Pignier, he published a book: *Method of Writing Words, Music, and Plain Songs by Means of Dots, for Use by the Blind and Arranged for Them.* The version of Braille explained in this book is essentially the same one that's used today.

Q: When was the Braille system of reading and writing officially adopted?

A: Students at the Royal Institute for Blind Youth in Paris began using Braille immediately, but it wasn't officially adopted there until 1854, two years after Louis's death. By that time, the use of Braille had spread throughout Europe and also to North America. Its formal implementation, however, was gradual and happened faster in Europe. The United States did not adopt Braille officially until 1932.

Q: What else did Louis invent?

A: Louis published books on the use of Braille in music, mathematics, and mapping. With the help of his friend Alexandre Fournier, he developed *raphigraphy* (also called *decapoint*), a system that allowed blind and sighted people to write to each other. With Pierre Foucault, a blind musician and mechanic, Louis invented a typewriter-like machine for raphigraphy that was an early version of dot-matrix printing.

Q: What role did music play in Louis's life?

A: Louis mastered the cello and the organ and played the latter professionally at two major churches in Paris. He also tuned pianos near Coupvray. Because musicianship was one of the few professional options for the blind, and because the sighted community had few objections to it, Louis made it a priority to develop his system of musical notation. As a result, his musical code gained widespread acceptance almost immediately.

Q: What happened after Louis finished his studies?

A: After completing his own education, Louis remained in Paris and became an assistant teacher at the Royal Institute for Blind Youth. In 1833, he became a full professor and taught history, rammar, geography, and math. After being diagnosed with (incurable) tuberculosis, he continued to teach, returning occasionally to his family home to rest and to visit. He died two days after his forty-third birthday and was buried in Coupvray. In 1952, the one hundredth anniversary of his death, his body was moved to the Panthéon in Paris, the final resting place of France's greatest men and women.

Q: How has Braille kept pace with the digital age?

A: Advances in technology have dramatically improved the number and kind of devices that visually impaired individuals can use to read and write. Access to these specialized devices remains a challenge, however, one that organizations such as the American Foundation for the Blind, the National Federation of the Blind, and the National Library Service for the Blind and Physically Handicapped continue to address. Some examples include: *electronic Braille note takers,* which provide an alternative to the traditional slate and stylus; *Braille display technology,* which provides information in Braille about what appears on a computer screen; *Braille printers,* which produce information from computer devices in hard copy; and *digital libraries,* where patrons can borrow books and magazines in Braille and in audio, as well as books that can be read by both sighted and blind individuals. Many smartphones and tablets also provide options for converting standard text to speech or to Braille.

TO LEARN MORE ABOUT LOUIS BRAILLE:

Bryant, Jennifer F. *Louis Braille: Teacher of the Blind.* New York: Chelsea House, 1994.

Freedman, Russell. *Out of Darkness: The Story of Louis Braille.* New York: Clarion Books, 1997.

Mellor, C. Michael. *Louis Braille: A Touch of Genius.* Boston: National Braille Press, 2006.

afb.org/louisbraillemuseum: thorough summary of Braille's life and work, with archival images and photographs.

books.google.com/books?id=V_O3x1E2Xe8C: link to the script of the dramatic play *Braille: The Early Life of Louis Braille* by Lola H. Jennings and Coleman A. Jennings. Woodstock, IL: Dramatic Publishing, 1989.

braillebug.org: teaches sighted children about Braille and gives links for educators and parents.

coupvray.fr: French-language site with visitors' information, directions, links, and photos of Braille's home in Coupvray.

TO LEARN MORE ABOUT USING BRAILLE:

Jeffrey, Laura S. *All About Braille: Reading by Touch.* Berkeley Heights, NJ: Enslow Publishers, 2004.

afb.org: The American Foundation for the Blind "removes barriers, creates solutions, and expands possibilities so people with vision loss can achieve their full potential."

loc.gov/nls/reference/factsheets/braille.html: The National Library Service for the Blind and Physically Handicapped, Library of Congress, provides a free-loan program for Braille and recorded books and magazines.

nbp.org: The National Braille Press is a nonprofit publisher that promotes literacy and information access for blind children.

nfb.org: The National Federation of the Blind "advocates for the civil rights and equality of blind Americans, and develops innovative education, technology, and training programs."

pbskids.org/arthur/print/braille: Marc Brown's Arthur character educates young people about blindness. Pages include an instant Braille translator.

To my agent, Alyssa E. Henkin—you're the best!
—J.B.

ACKNOWLEDGMENTS

Our deepest gratitude to the following people and organizations for their help in shaping this book: Allison Wortche and Nancy Siscoe, editors at Knopf; Artie Bennett, eagle-eyed copy editor; Sarah Hokanson, designer; Barbara Perris, translator; Alyssa E. Henkin, literary agent, Trident Media Group; Elizabeth Burns, youth services consultant, NJ State Library Talking Book & Braille Center; Patricia Maurer, director of reference, Jacobus tenBroek Library, Jernigan Institute, National Federation of the Blind; Deborah Kendrick, senior features editor, *AccessWorld,* American Foundation for the Blind; Dr. Rebecca H. Ward, ophthalmologist.

THIS IS A BORZOI BOOK PUBLISHED BY ALFRED A. KNOPF

Text copyright © 2016 by Jen Bryant • Jacket art and interior illustrations copyright © 2016 by Boris Kulikov

All rights reserved. Published in the United States by Alfred A. Knopf, an imprint of Random House Children's Books, a division of Penguin Random House LLC, New York. Knopf, Borzoi Books, and the colophon are registered trademarks of Penguin Random House LLC.

Visit us on the Web! randomhousekids.com

Educators and librarians, for a variety of teaching tools, visit us at RHTeachersLibrarians.com

Library of Congress Cataloging-in-Publication Data is available upon request.
ISBN 978-0-449-81337-9 (trade) — ISBN 978-0-449-81338-6 (lib. bdg.) — ISBN 978-0-449-81339-3 (ebook)

The illustrations in this book were created using mixed media.
MANUFACTURED IN CHINA   September 2016   10 9 8 7 6 5 4 3 2 1   First Edition
Random House Children's Books supports the First Amendment and celebrates the right to read.